Mouth Toward Sky

poems by

Geraldine Foote

Finishing Line Press
Georgetown, Kentucky

Mouth Toward Sky

Copyright © 2018 by Geraldine Foote
ISBN 978-1-63534-601-5 First Edition
All rights reserved under International and Pan-American Copyright Conventions. No part of this book may be reproduced in any manner whatsoever without written permission from the publisher, except in the case of brief quotations embodied in critical articles and reviews.

ACKNOWLEDGMENTS

The author thanks the following publications where these poems or earlier versions have appeared:

Chaparral Poetry Forum, Redrock Writers, March 2005, "Greg, Gone Fishing"
Clark College Poetry Contest Anthology, May, 1994: Honorable Mention Clark College Contest (OSPA,WSPA). "Half Moon: At the Ocean Without My Son"
The English Journal, 1986, "Still Learning My Colors at 33"
Icarus: One Small Step, December 2002, "Afterlife"
The Moose, A Magazine of Portland Poetry, April, 1981, "At Sea"
North Coast Times Eagle, August-September 2002, "History Lesson"; October, 2003 "Imagine This"
The Oregonian, September 1984,"History Lesson"; June 1998, "After the Letter"
Peace, Peace to the Far, and to the Near, 2006, anthology of poems from the exhibit, Trinity Episcopal Cathedral, "Imagine This"
Poets Against the War (http://www.poetsagainstthewar.org/), July 22, 2005 Poem of the Week, "Imagine This"
Portland Lights: A Poetry Anthology, eds. LaMorticella, Nemerov, Fall, 1999,"Vi, Like Pie"
Reed College Exile, Spring, 1981,"Possessed Place"
The Southwest Connection, September 2002, reprinted "My Father's Flag"
VoiceCatcher, Summer 2014, "And the King Was in the Counting House"

Publisher: Leah Maines
Editor: Christen Kincaid
Cover Art: Debby Neely
Author Photo: Lifetouch
Cover Design: Elizabeth Maines McCleavy

Printed in the USA on acid-free paper.
Order online: www.finishinglinepress.com
also available on amazon.com

Author inquiries and mail orders:
Finishing Line Press
P. O. Box 1626
Georgetown, Kentucky 40324
U. S. A.

Table of Contents

Junior High German Class 1963 1
My Imaginary Life with an American Tragedy 2
Afterlife 3
Possessed Place 4
Repatriation 5
At Sea 6
The Man Is a Metaphor 7
History Lesson 8
Still Learning My Colors at 33 9
For A Man Who Loves Mountains 10
Sap of Birches 12
Greg? Gone Fishing 13
Drinking Rain 14
Going to the Wall 15
Vi, Like Pie 16
Official Notice 18
After the Letter 19
Covenant 20
Half Moon 21
Advent: After Our Fathers Die 22
Scar Line 24
My Father's Flag 25
Imagine This 26
Sweeping the Passage 27
International Women's Day 28
And the King Was in the Counting House 30
Bridging the Distance 31

Junior High German Class 1963

After the bell, we girls spent that lunch hour
in the restroom, crying, until
an announcement came to let us go home early.

This was after the radio news had come over the speaker box
at the start of German class and our first *wie gehts* of the day.

Some of us had giggled—thinking a sneaky
office aide had flipped the switch behind
the secretary's back, sending Jan and Dean or
the Beach Boys through the intercom, then words
and static sunk in—*Dallas* and
President—froze our smiles.
We weren't sure how to act.

In seventh grade, where we had learned what it meant
when our President said *Ich bin ein Berliner!*,
our laughter faded
into the map-lined walls, our fragile
weltanchaung reformed.

My Imaginary Life with an American Tragedy

Home that long weekend, I learned the word
cortege, heard the slow drum....

While advent came and went,
over and over I heard *ask not*....

In bed before sleep, I prayed he'd
come back, dreamed they'd only *told* us
he had died, while, in a protected location,
surgeons performed magic on his brain.
Not even Jackie had been told, in order
to make the ruse that he had died more real.

Once our President recovered, we would
forgive the conspiracy, shout our *danke's*
while Jack & Jackie strolled the beach barefoot,
sehr schön, wind mussing their hair.

Then, when too long a time had passed,
I hoped, *bitte*, for reincarnation, impatient
for a hero. We girls no longer aspired
to be first lady, nor President,

and the stories I penned
ended in tragic clichés—
heroines died or their surfer heartthrobs drowned—
those left behind facing *das Leid* with stoic strength.

Afterlife

After his death, she kept finding
these hairs, in the tub, curled and black
like eyelashes or little crescent moons
on the bathroom counter, in the sink.
She should have hired a cleaning lady—
at least for a time, she thought to herself,
then, *no, it's better this way,*

*now I have something to do...something to
save.* She picked them
one by one, from the sink, the shower floor;
they gleamed and winked from the white
porcelain of the toilet. Carefully collected,
they lay curled in the jewel box
next to the baby teeth of their only son.

Tonight these moons speak in a language she believes
tells her to grieve is human, to love divine.
She prays to forget. She prays not to forget.
She counts eyelashes in a box
she had forgotten, remembering,
then missing, his socks
on the bathroom floor.

Possessed Place

Sometimes I still look out that second floor
window and down at the tiled pool. I watch
leaves swoosh into piles at one end,
see dandelions pushing through cracks
in tiled walkways nobody walks
and wonder why she died so young.

> She gets careless,
> *or else I made her up,*
> forgets to return things,
> *or I just left them somewhere.*
> The neighbor said the child screamed
> and he ran over, too late. The tiled pool
> was never filled again.
>
> Sometimes, we both
> live there. She gets careless, leaves
> tell-tale signs: knocks over a plant, breaks
> glass, but never casts a bad spell over my
> place like my man the night I see him
> pushing me over the stairs—he has
> both hands on my neck. I hear *her* cry,
> gulp for air.

He stopped
when he saw I saw
the look of his eyes.
And I left for good
the comfort
of objects moved or missing,

and the pool that filled each morning with eerie
watching—the crack in the shallow end—and wondering
if the child's father
had swung at it, hard, with iron,
before he moved away.

Repatriation
    for Ida

I am in exile from her yellow kitchen,
the linoleum floor catching her coffee drips,
the Formica table, cool to the touch with
ridges and balls of chrome I can see
myself in. In exile from her hands

red with berries, her tea towel
twisting, full of seeds, squeezing juice
for jam or jelly. I am denied: her
back porch, the roll out clothesline,
ships passing three streets below
while we feed neighborhood strays,
hang our shirts and sandy jeans.

Time keeps the sheets we sent into her backyard sky…

Only this poem repatriates me to Grandpa Paul's
silent radio, the empty rocker alongside, tall firs
out the kitchen window, that hid secrets at certain
dusk, a dark dread that sent me wandering

to the cool basement with its wheelbarrow
and woodpile, washer wringing shirts
slowly out onto the stone floor,
the dirty four-paned windows
that let in too little light

except in morning when it came
streaming in from the river below,
exposing cobwebs, the fear of bats.

At Sea

Oceans,
I want oceans, not
oceans of feeling
drowning me with each new love.

Breezes,
like fingers in hair, not hands,
just air's caress, not holding.

And holding,
as branches hold birds
not the grasping of one
or many hands
human and not…

And wave
upon wave of sand
with gritty protest,
under human feet,
to be the only sound, I want
my human feet to yield,
sink into wet,
and sandcastles, not dreams,
be the only homes destroyed.

Let Ocean at night
be the only sound
in murmured distance
as I sleep to dream,
wave upon wave destroyed,
reborn at sea,
always reborn,
always at sea.

The Man Is a Metaphor
for John Lennon

And I hardly knew you, only knew you
stepping from a plane in sixty-four,
knew you as snatches of songs, words
sending waves across oceans, starting
something, over and over again for the rock,
for peace; magician casting birds whose beaks
peck revolution in disks, turning convolutions, risking
spirals, leading somehow forward and out of the past.

And last night I dreamed, and I did not
dream your death. In fact,
you weren't even in the dream.
There was a fish though.

I was bitten. I was standing, my feet
gripping the gritty bottom of the sea.
In waist deep eddies, I steadied myself
on a barnacled rock with one hand.
The other hand floated in water, when the fish
not large, passing my sinking place, bit me
and left a half moon mark on my hand.

And on my death bed—was I dying?—
or on my sick bed, I lay, and a man came.
He spoke of bodies and rolling rivers,
beauty, and bodies, long and lithe.
But he was a friend, I suppose,
and you and I, John, we're not friends,
except in a pool of notes and words,
out there where we are sometimes bitten.

History Lesson

Class, I must apologize
for the film we are about to see.
If you would like to be excused,
I will give you a pass to the library.
If you have a weak stomach, you may
wish to be excused.
> *I cannot be held responsible*
> *for any sudden loss of innocence.*
>
> *I cannot be held responsible*
> *after the rain, or when the skin slips*
> *off like a glove, or when you see*
> *the person without a mouth.*

You will be responsible for anything I write on the blackboard:
> 50,000 dead instantly w/in 10 miles of center
> 100,000 dead later w/in 50 miles of center
> Today's bombs: 200,000 X Hiroshima, Nagasaki

> *And you will*
> *be held responsible for the knowledge.*

Still Learning My Colors at 33
for Tye

I first knew chartreuse when Alice,
whose man drums for a rock and roll band, asked me to
bring her something chartreuse to wear from San Francisco.
Have to admit, I wasn't even sure how it looked, though I
liked the sound of the word in her attic room. Chartreuse
"...sort of a lemon-lime...
not lime green," she said, "not yellow...
something in between. You'll know when you see it.
There's nothing like it."

I didn't like the idea; this
yellow-green had me thinking fingernails on a blackboard.
I thought Alice a little crazy, had visions of her painting her
fingernails chartreuse, maybe even wearing
chartreuse tights lit by blacklights, between
dances, sipping her liqueur, miraculously
tasting of the same color.

And yesterday, standing before the waterfall
you showed me moss
brushed with a light   quick   stroke to amaze
(there's nothing like it)
chartreuse in the flood of day's true
light and water, falling to nurture
chartreuse on the rocks.

For a Man Who Loves Mountains

I'd never seen the great blue heron before I met you,
then you flew into my life from Mount Olympus,
or wherever the souls of mountain men come from,
and things began to happen,
like the full moon December night
when the sea sprinkled sand pennies,
                    love tokens from Neptune,
and the white sand dollar stars and the moon
lit the smile around your eyes, lit the shells,
and we skipped in winter waters unafraid,
knowing anything with a name like velella velella,
by-the-wind sailor, or
          aurelia aurita, with its sand dollar shape afloat,
could not be the dread jellyfish of our childhoods.

If anyone had seen us that night, they would have thought us
possessed, prancing, up to our knees in surf and moonlight,
straining to see tiny sand dollars we called pennies.

I decided it meant we were blessed, and stayed
                    with you, knowing we'd find more.

Since then, we've found
shells enough to make ten thimbles out of baby owl limpets
and a periwinkle ring for the pot that holds the hoya plant from
Grandma Ida's back porch. The china caps,
which are limpets you like to call mountains,
create miniature topography on the top of our television set.
We need a relief map to keep track of our treasures.

You say sand dollars have *eccentricus* in their scientific name, and I say
appropriate, since one often finds them
          on the shelves of eccentrics who want to feel rich.

If I start to feel guilty,
you tell me some people collect countries, instead of
searching for moon snails or the purple olive snail
I'd like to find, with you, and make escargot
and serve it with wine
to all of the people who have ever loved you,
if they like escargot,
and to all of your enemies, if they don't.

For now, we savor the awe we feel
for the time we saw the heron...at dusk...and crept close,
so I could say I'd been five feet from a stick that finally became a heron,
and you could say you read it in a book how herons were hated by hunters
because they sentineled for the ducks.
                                              And I was proud
                                the great blue heron
whose wingspan reaches through skies in my mind
let you
come so close.

Sap of Birches

Suppose the clothes washed themselves, hung themselves, the toys
knew their places, the shoes refused to go beyond the stoop.

Suppose time were just as long as the moment's joy demands,
just as short as the wish of the shot,
and artists, not accountants, figured the tax
based upon the rule of poets who assume their
rightful places as legislators of human aspiration.

Then would we outlaw despair? Leave it to waste
away in a damp cellar, the dank smell drifting up
only on the occasion of a hairy hag's reminder of baseness,
that we may know the value of smooth-skinned hope
bounding in the meadow.

Suppose, just before each full moon,
women could drink the sap of birches
to see them through the wanings.
Suppose men raised roses into the air,
scented petals the only casualties of battle.

Suppose the ghosts of beaten children
could sing their tormentors to permanent sleep,
then assume flesh, cradled in the longing
arms of the infertile made new.

Greg? Gone fishing...

Smile, the memory: his feet in the waders...
I thought he meant tall boots, not these
rubber overalls with feet like child's pajamas,
rubbered toes stuffed inside torn hightops,
holes in places his feet want out.

Shoes that old
must carry safety in them,
in the waders, warmth...even under this
weathered sky, above our campsite—
clouds, phantom blue, fears
and wishes trailing white robes.

Greg? Gone fishing.
When I ask where his mind goes
when he fishes in his waders, he
can't say. He thinks. He fishes.

His casts take him beyond trees
so I imagine him: head bending
over his hand, cupped, holding
the flies he has tied by lamplight, choosing
the river, larks singing. Wings stitch
leitmotif bank to bank,
the never ceasing
undercurrent, riverbeat,
rushing applause for the man,
for the growing green,
for the pole with its singular
tentacle above the swoosh of water on stone—
a wand or a whip, a willow, he waves it, soundless—
shimmering.

Drinking Rain

Mom, you know what? I can drink rai......n,
he announces, at three, nearly singing *rain.*

I just go to the place where the rain is,
and then I open my mouth
and I put my mouth toward the sky
                          —he leans his head back—
and the RAIN...FALLS...IN...

He draws out the *in* on a high note,
hands to each side, palms to the sky,
as if to say
how simple it is.

Going to the Wall

If I went to the wall I would weep,
not because I had gone to that war myself,
or knew to look for the particular name of someone who had
but because in the fatal sum of those grooved
names glistening in rain,
the dying ideal no longer scents the air,
cut rose dried in the gradual
graying of possible blue
or a more sudden gossamer
whisked away
to see clearly how we have failed, together,
each shining example,
one name
on the wall…
and another name, not.

Vi, Like Pie

Vi...et...nam, he whispers, reading a green road sign.
Then, loudly, from the passenger side,
...*Mom, what's Vi-et-nam?*
I ask him to repeat it;
I'm busy looking at fallen trees, days after a freak ice storm,
and he's saying vi like pie;
it takes a couple of tries before I understand
he's seen *Vietnam Memorial* on the sign
for the turn to the Oregon Zoo.

"Vietnam is a country in Asia," I say, my throat clogged...seeing
friends tormented by buddies with belly wounds they will
not forget. Apprehension throbs,
in morning fog, warnings crack like tree limbs; this
could be a quagmire of questions, so soon,
icicles fall with the melting, too soon
must he know. Breathe...

then words tumble out, sporadic: "...a war,
I was a teen; young men, my age and Daddy's, as young as 18 or
20...fought there. Some died." When I pause for air,
he stops me, suddenly attentive. *Some died?*
"...some were from here, so people built a memorial,
this big wall, and put all their names on it, up near the zoo."

I think of taking him there, but not now;
when we go, it will be overcast, with the promise
of sun, shafts through clouds, not this blue-skinned ice,
the soggy possibility of trees above our heads losing ground.

How many of them died?
He asks for numbers, too soon.
I'm surprised to be no longer sure.

"50,000, I think."
How many went?
"...I, I think over 500,000,
and 50,000 died, but I'm not sure."

He's silent a moment, counting, while I count trees, newly split, stabbing grey sky. *That's half of them*, he says.
"Well, no," I say, gently, and help him do the math.

Official Notice

She reads each word twice.
Still the words do not link arms to deliver the sense.

Her husband takes the letter,
crisp and white with a seal at the top embossed in gold.
He sits down on the plaid sofa and reads.

She stands at the picture window, notices
how the squirrel has chewed the sides of the bird feeder,

notices dandelions
in the grass that shouts for a mower
pushed by someone young and strong.

She gazes for a long time, confused
that the sun should come now
to dance light on a rain-washed world.

After the Letter

The fields lie fallow,
all has been plowed under.
A rich, dark loam clings
to the soles of his workboots,
scenting the air.

Every day, he walks these fields
with a hesitating step,
pausing now and then for breath.
He does not falter.
The windmill turns slowly.

The barn stands, weathered
wood too far gone for paint.
The door hangs right on its
hinges; the roof, watertight,
at a price.

The scarecrow needs redress—
its tattered coat will not last the winter.
Stuffing lies scattered at its feet.

On the porch, the footlocker
rusts, unopened. Rain and sun
thrust light, parting clouds.
He leans on the post, gazing.
An empty rocker

sways as if just deserted.
Paint chips off on his hand.
He is surprised that it is yellow;
Something cheery, she had said,
like butter melting in the sun.

Covenant

Backlit by sinking sun,
one glorious evening before rain at sea,
the tall boy, inviting music, mimes the arts of conductors,
raised arms stringed to a sky bird, then a sand bird, grounded, dragged.
Up again, kite like a dream,
orchestrated by breeze, forth and back, across covenant sky.

Time and again, vigilance relaxes—kite-bird turns
bomber by an errant draft, until hands, in shifting wind,
human hands, invite breath to
honor a fragile compact,
revive
the heavenly dance.

Half Moon: At the Ocean Without My Son

> In my mind I warn you not to touch jellyfish
> even when they look like ice sculptures
> time has frozen.

Sometimes I want to freeze you
now that you're no longer small enough to hold
in one hand.

> You are still small enough to lift
> (just barely and not very high)
> and small enough to rest in my lap,
> head on my chest until

sandboxes and airplanes, helicopters and trucks
send you running from me
like the choo-choo trains winding through our living room.

When the sand squeaks beneath my feet it says *Nathan Nathan* again
and I wonder if I've shown you how to shuffle your feet to make this
sound.

A mound of sand, once a sandcastle, built by a child older than you,
is populated by the webbed prints of gulls now absent, and I
think of your small feet

kicking with glee
the turrets I have built.

Advent: After Our Fathers Die
For Linda

In the woods as we walk, I'm telling you how I
wept in the pew today,
how that hymn that says, *I was there*
        to hear your bourning cry...had *me* crying.
Along the winding trail, I'm telling you
about the mother in church
who is now without her son,
and how the congregation sang the hymn, how *I* sang
haltingly and thought about *my* son
sitting beside me while her son is not.
While my father is not and your father,
not sitting beside you, and how
walking this path, we are both
without our fathers now,
singing that part about middle age,
whatever comes next, in the hymn I was
too choked to sing, wondering if I ever
could ask for, hear, such a song...
thinking this *ridiculous* because
my son could never *not* be there...in my life,
with me still singing.

By now I'm sobbing on a bench,
surrounded by moss, telling you
how I cried, I'm crying, because I know he'll
go on without me...just as we are now,
minus our fathers; I won't be around to see....

Cold and wet, with no Kleenex, under rain-
dipped trees, almost keening *don't you see*
someday he might sit sobbing among dripping fir...
might breathe cold air in great gulps.

In the forest chill, you and I are both crying and
laughing until we ache, soggy, and I
tell you about the time he was

sniffling in the car, asking for tissue, with me
searching my pockets, my purse, under the seat
until he laughed through tears and said, *A good mom
would have tissue*, and this became our joke
replayed again and again.

I'm backing up now, explaining how during the hymn,
I wanted to put my arm around him,
brimming with possibility there in the pew,
knowing he, too, might
choke on this rough pit. That's all.

And sometimes I dare look deep into this creek,
beyond the bank of shoe-sucking mud, to see clearly
rocks which are stones which have given in
until they are smooth as touchstones...

This walk in the great green moist...
tears cold on the face of our friendship?
I know with my whole soul the loving,
the losing it takes, to learn what I have,
what to count, until the next loss propels us
down this forested path again,
trusting to this grace my only son.

Scar Line
    after a line by William Stafford.

They tell the slant life takes, these scars
that have no time for worry before
accident flies into the path of
children, mothers, the body
propelled faster than feet into space,
gravity wins and the child's chin
meets the floor in sudden indelible conflict.

                      This knee scar
tells her she was careless in youth, attests to
the new blue Schwinn making wind, pinned
playing cards slap slapping too fast
on spokes turning, applause for the child
who rides fear-less-ly free, wind
in her hair, wind in her feet flying on pedals until scree

                      scatters, wheels skid.
Her son has a thin line near his crown,
where he flew blind, chased,
swooping under the playground bridge,
his feet leaving no time to gauge how
low to duck his head or discover
how tall he had grown in a year.

                      Along the shaved spot,
her fingers still trace the flight
along the freeway from work,
bloody head wound gaping above white
knuckles on the wheel,
the red splash
no mere paint makes on a white shirt,

how grace reminds the living
with a thin line
on a small scalp, taunting.

My Father's Flag
    9/14/01

I tell you I want to hang my father's flag.
People have died, thousands.
It is a time for flags.

My mother has given it to me, the flag they gave her
a year-and-a-half-ago when he died, a veteran of world war.

Driving from store to store for a bracket and
pole to hang the flag, I find them all sold out.
I think of hanging it from gutters or eaves, but it is too long—
the American flag must never touch the ground.

I try a long stick of bamboo, but the flag
is too heavy, the pole bends like a willow
and the flag almost brushes the ground unless I
drape it across my shoulders.

The flag is too large, too heavy a cloth
to be hung from our home. I am almost glad.
If it flew, I'd want to hang a banner with a dove
alongside, lest I be misunderstood. And I don't have one.

You help me fold the flag, to put it away, and we remember
how we learned this protocol in ceremonies at our childhood
camps. We promise each other we will teach our son,
who is not a Scout, how to fold the flag.

We make each loving fold until my father's flag,
and the liberty for which it stands, is a triangle
to hold against my aching heart.

Imagine This

Imagine the ghosts of Arlington
gathered in Congress to say they
know the answer does not
lie in bayonets and dirty bombs,
empty skies moaning with drones.

Imagine the possibilities
in sky, in blue with a few wisps
of cloud, and Einstein telling us
what equals what and whom
we should die for; imagine

living instead, imagine
meadows in the craters, paintings
in caves brought to light,
the deep sound of thought,
brushing against the truth of it
and pens scratching
like beaks of extinct birds
reminding us
of the past pointing
to this future.

Sweeping the Passage

When you leave, I'll sweep the floor clean.
Tiny beads of rubber from the turf field will fall
from the shoes you leave behind
peppering the floor of your past for awhile
and I'll have to sweep again and again
with less to irritate each time,
missing you on the couch with your guitar,
until perhaps I won't sweep at all, just leave
one or two for your return.

The lacrosse stick you leave behind
won't trip me anymore. I'll
be able to put it
in its place
and it will stay
out of the way until you visit.

Yes, in this, your home,
you will become a visitor (and not)
and when you're away, I'll swing the stick
you once used to rescue a sparrow
perched high in our house, I'll swing it
forward, then side to side, half a twirl,
hard and fast to remind myself
of the whoosh of your passage.

International Women's Day 3/8/17

You turn to look at me, so I
make believe I'm not there.

I can live at the bottom of a well.
I know how to sink and swim.

You build castles on sand.
I still sail the moat.

You lock doors out of fear.
I open to let the dog out.

You give as little as possible. I
pay the tax with increasing regret.

You paint the world black and white,
while I'm at the age of grey.

Like marshmallows, you eat my
optimism. I set fire

to pessimism like a bush.
When you say I whine too much,

I shut my mouth for five days.
Then I practice quiet shouting

and loud listening. Who walks without
marching and stoops to the minute?

I have found stones
in my shoes once too often.

You are delighted when I stumble.
 I pick myself up, going first to my knees.

You separate my roots. I search
for a family plot.

I cannot open my life
without a can opener.

Inside rotting plums, you grow
platitudes I refuse to eat.

And when you say I can't,
I say I can, and I name

disbelief a sneaky thief.
We can lie down to resist

or we can lie down to rest,
but who wants to lie

and lie in the ground forever?
You have changed me, and I

allow hate to burn my hands.
Who dives into the net, while

I rise, while I rise? I cannot fly
with my heels taped to the ground.

And the King Was in the Counting House
Frenzy of fear likely dropped 3,000 birds. —AP 1/4/11

On the day the blackbirds fell from the sky, some spun
like pinwheels, others flew blind into the sides of tall buildings.
One struck a woman out walking her dog, which barked
incessantly and tried to retrieve the winged carcass as she lay there.
Convoys swerved to avoid feathered lumps littering the road
and small red-winged missiles pummeled hoods and windshields.

No, these are not the demanding crows,
feathers slicked and strutting all shiny. These
black birds are smaller, delicate,
pinned with red flags like medals on their wings,
greeting morning in phosphorus-like flashes. At dusk,
they're tiny drones swooping in for twilight soirees at the roost.

The blackbirds were struck by lightening
or stressed by the midnight explosions of revelers.
Ringing a new year, the people became oblivious
to how much this looks like the old year,
not even seeing the winged ones striking ground,
then staggering drunk to their deaths, become collateral.

At first, the people thought Hitchcock's "The Birds" had come,
or the End Times, and they shunned the bodies piling up,
running home to embrace and huddle with loved ones.
The redwings, startled, in a frenzy of fear, flew, they say,
despite poor eyesight, disoriented in dark, their trembling
breasts bursting amid pyrotechnics or the blunt force trauma of thunder.

A few unfortunates crashed beak-first into ground,
not so dignified in death, not photographed, acknowledged
or embraced; far more than four and twenty baked
in an American pie, these delicate casualties
shoved, warm, into the corner of time's cupboard
become a contented fiction.

Bridging the Distance

I heard a whale breathing,
last night in the gathering dark,
the water darker but shining far out,
between this island
and the one across the channel
in the rippling, distant dark,

deep breaths,
undertones in the undertow,
and wet breath blowing spray
above the darkest
of the distant black shines.

To ask you to listen,
I came inside the cabin,
and there you sprawled
asleep, not quite upright
on the couch, head back,
mouth open, your breath
a wet, spent drone and whish.

Was this what I heard
by water just now? You,
throwing your sound

all the way to that far island
and back again to me,
the distance
between us,
at last, traversed.

Additional Acknowledgments

Many thanks to Dianne Stepp and Marvin Bell for their encouragement and advice, to the Odds Poetry Group for their comments on countless poems over the years, to the faculty of the Pacific University MFA for their generous sharing of craft in the many talks I have been honored to hear while volunteering, and to my husband and son, Greg & Nate Fritts, who enrich my life and these poems.

In addition, the following poems were chosen by students for publication in *Polyglot*, Literary and Arts Magazine, Lincoln High School, where the author taught for 22 years: "Official Notice"(2005); "Imagine This" (2004); "My Father's Flag" (2002); "Drinking Rain" (2000); "Sap of Birches"(1999); "Going to the Wall (1998); "For A Man Who Loves Mountains," 1994.

A fourth-generation Oregonian, **Geraldine** was born in Portland, where she has lived most of her life. She spent her grade school years in Santa Rosa, California and, while in high school, was an exchange student in New Delhi, India. She attended Stanford in the late 60s and early 70s where she became involved in work against the Vietnam War and war research on campus. After years at San Jose State and Portland State universities, she earned a B.S. degree in History, and eventually, an M.A.L.S. degree from Reed College with a creative thesis in poetry. For over twenty years, Geraldine developed and taught in high school writing programs and later helped to found the low residency MFA in Writing program at Pacific University.

Known to friends and family as Gerry, she currently divides her time between family, writing, art, singing, and peace and justice advocacy work. The latter includes co-direction of the Veterans Bridge Fund to assist those returned from deployments, and work in support of a shelter for victims of domestic violence. She recently became a steward for Menucha, a non-profit artist and retreat center in the Columbia River Gorge.

Gerry enjoys hiking or kayaking along the Oregon Coast, Orcas Island, and Northwest rivers with husband, Greg, and son, Nathan, both fly-fishermen. While they fish, she paddles, writes, and paints miniature watercolors, capturing images for her poems and for use in *Peace Leaves*, a series of gift poems, letter-pressed editions on leaf-shaped fine arts papers, sold in bookstores and galleries. A few of the poems in this book contain lines that found their way into *Peace Leaves* editions, as does her children's poem *Child, You Are*, available in a limited edition hand-sewn book from the author.

Geraldine has been honored for her poetry by the Oregon Council of Teachers of English, Soapstone, Poets Against the War, and the Oregon Poetry Association. Her poems have appeared in publications that include *The English Journal; Sunrust; The Oregonian; Fireweed; The Reed College Exile; Voicecatcher; Four and Twenty Poetry;* as well as the anthologies *Inquiry: The Immigrant Experience; Peace, Peace to* the Far, and to the Near; Raising Our Voices; Icarus: One Small Step; and *Portland Lights*.

Of her life and work the author states: *I am witness in a changing world, exploring my roots as a fourth generation Oregonian and living my role as steward for a fifth, mining a familiar northwest landscape for metaphor and meaning. Drawing upon what nature teaches, I hope to inspire, teach myself and others to live lovingly in a changing world, remind us of our shared humanity.*

www.ingramcontent.com/pod-product-compliance
Lightning Source LLC
LaVergne TN
LVHW040117080426
835507LV00041B/1261